How to Podcast When You Aren't Tech Savvy

A Clear-Cut Book about How (and Why) to Launch a Podcast

Casey Callanan

DEDICATION

This book is for all the underdogs out there.
Podcasting is your medium.

CONTENTS

ACKNOWLEDGMENTS

Thank you to everyone who helped make this dream possible.
I hope you know who you are.

CHAPTER 1
WHY I WROTE THIS BOOK

My parents live close to a very prestigious University on the East Coast of the United States. My cousin, who works there, once invited me to a free workshop for undergraduate students about how to start a podcast. She knew I was a podcaster and understood how much I value learning. She invited me to check it out.

Having hosted, edited and marketed a successful podcast for more than a year at the time, I wasn't exactly the intended audience.

However, I like to keep my ego in check and maintain an open mind, so I thought it'd still be a great idea.

It was for beginner-level podcasters, but I figured it'd be nice to get back on a college campus and soak up that environment a bit. I assumed there'd be a couple nuggets of quality information I could take away from the evening. It could help me podcast better.

I may have gone in with the right mindset, but I immediately became discouraged by the instructor. He made it seem so complicated. He went into details about sound theory and audio engineering. It was pure cognitive overload. I got really frustrated. This was way above what beginners should be learning, and frankly it was unnecessary.

This was a voluntary class for ambitious young people eager to learn. They wanted to spread their messages and get their voices heard through a podcast. Sadly, I could tell this one bad teacher was ruining it for them. They took diligent notes, but it was just too much unnecessary content for them to absorb. The looks on their faces said it all.

I guarantee these kids left this seminar discouraged and did not start a podcast. I say this because more than half the room left in the middle of this workshop.

The experience hit a personal nerve within me. It got me thinking about when I was a student and how quality teachers could make or break everything. The role of the teacher is so crucial. Bad teachers produce bad outcomes. I learned later in life that the antidote to a bad teacher is a strong will.

When it comes to learning about how to launch a podcast, you have to have an unbreakable will that one bad teacher doesn't stand a chance against. Get resourceful. Meet people. Ask questions. Read. Most importantly of all, actually do it. Follow through with the steps outlined in this book and get the podcast published.

I want to issue a fair warning to any critics out there that say the steps to launch a great podcast are far more complicated than I make it out to be. This book is meant to get you from someone who has no clue about how to do it, to someone who has a podcast up on iTunes and available to the world.

That is how we are going to define success. For people stuck in permanent "analysis paralysis" torture, yes there are a million little things that can be done to perfect the podcast. However, this book is not about perfection. It's about making something out of nothing; thus, our theme is, "Done is Better Than Perfect".

The more you try and do something, the more success and confidence will come your way. Podcasting, like golf, standup comedy, and many other pursuits, is something you can work at improving upon your entire life. It's never too late to take it on and the more you do it, the better you'll get.

My Story

I am a writer and an artist. There was a time when the last thing I wanted to do was waste precious time learning technology when I could have been working on my art form. I just wanted to create.

When I was in college studying journalism, all I wanted to do was interview my sources and write.

I did not want to learn about (or do) anything else academically. Once my elective courses were out of the way, I had pure tunnel vision to learn my craft and get better at it. I was very stubborn.

I have a theory. People who supposedly hate technology or feel as though they aren't tech savvy have other skill sets that few other people possess. They don't want to take the time to learn the steps that are necessary to master or be comfortable with technology. They'd rather just do what they're good at. In my case, I would rather have been writing.

In high school with computers, all I was required to know was how to turn it on and use Microsoft Word. All I knew in college was how to open a word document and start writing. And that's all I wanted to do. I felt that learning how to be a great writer and report stories as a journalist was hard enough. I didn't want to allocate time learning anything else.

That mentality got me through college. Being able to write was enough. I always fell back on that number one core competency. I didn't have any interest at all in learning whatever else they tried to teach us.

They made valiant efforts to get us interested in web design. They tried to teach us how to lay out beautiful documents, and make magic with graphic design. They tried to increase our skill sets so we could be ready for a job in the real world. But I didn't apply myself to lesson plans on how to design fancy documents, shoot video, take great photography, etc. I didn't care. My calling was to write and report stories.

I could do all that in Microsoft Word I figured, so why bother learning anything else! (This was clearly an arrogant mindset in hindsight).

Then I graduated, and the real world hit me in the face.

I wasn't going to be able to simply interview people and write if I wanted to make a living. I couldn't skate by on my strong writing skills. There were simply no jobs! I had to learn technology.

I graduated when journalism jobs for recent college graduates were near impossible to find. If you wanted a job in media, you had to be creative in a multitude of different ways. You had to know web design, how to shoot and edit video. You had to have a surplus of other skill sets that went beyond what I knew how to do (write and report). If you even wanted just a sniff of a full-time job in media after college, you had to have some serious digital and design skills.

Living with my parents and reporting stories as a freelance journalist for a few local newspapers came next for me ($50 a week or so doing this didn't cut it). I also worked a part-time job doing something I could have done without a high school degree. It was humbling, and it helped me learn that just getting by on my writing was not going to cut it in the real world.

I really needed to learn technology, so I embraced it full on. I changed my attitude. It was all about my will. One of my favorite movies is *Rudy*; a story about an underdog football player at the University of Notre Dame. Rudy didn't have any size or talent, but he had the will. He wanted it more than the next guy.

His story had always inspired me, but this time I tried to apply it to life. I got that want. I *wanted* to learn technology and how to do things like creating awesome websites and killer podcasts.

I truly embraced this new media world we lived in. Becoming a writer, just a writer, in the marketplace that I was entering was impossible. So, I changed my attitude, and I developed a strong will to learn this stuff, and everything changed for the better.

I learned that I didn't hate technology. It was allowing me to be more creative than ever. I was able to get my ideas out to more people than ever. I learned the systems. It was easy to get the hang of technology when I applied myself. I got a great job in marketing where I was able to continue to use all of the communication skills that I loved. Everything was now sustainable.

It all changed with my attitude adjustment, and to be honest, facing the real world changed my attitude and got me thinking right. Sometimes lessons are learned best the hard way, but you don't need to have that rude awakening. Just take the time to learn these tiny pieces of tech and become a little web savvy.

For a prime example, you don't need to know what an RSS feed is in order to launch a podcast. You just have to find it under Settings in your free SoundCloud account. Then you copy and paste it into your free iTunes Connect account. (I'll outline these simple steps for you in Chapter 4).

I've embraced technology totally. Often it simply boils down to having the patience to search Google and then, read/follow the subsequent directions. You can figure out just about anything with that method.

Having the will to learn these basic steps to start a podcast is everything. Willpower leads those that are "stuck" to reach out to a friend who knows a little bit about technology. There are always ways to get things done in this digital world.

I find patience to be important. Resilience and patience will conquer your fears and doubt when it comes to launching a podcast. Having that will to ask questions to the people around you is crucial.

Podcasting doesn't involve a sophisticated amount of tech savvy to do it well, but you definitely can't "hate it" nor think it "hates you." It's your friend, and anyone can figure it out. Besides, it's the other skill sets inherent in you that are far more important, and that's your VOICE and your PASSION (you know, that thing you want to podcast about!)

Have the will to want to do this because once you learn those little steps, you'll realize that the real skill is the creative and authentic voice you bring to this podcast. The art of it separates you from everyone else. People who know how to use technology are a dime a dozen, but the unique voice that you can bring to a podcast is the real value we're trying to uncover.

Technology does not hate you. It treats everyone the same.

You don't have to be anything close to "tech savvy" to launch a podcast. Persistence, patience and a little resourcefulness will do the trick. Navigating audio editing software and using a podcast hosting website has never been easier, and it's widely available for free.

Unlike having a unique personality with something to say, being tech-savvy is not a key component of running a successful podcast.

Don't be intimidated about starting a podcast because they live on the internet and iPhones. Don't think twice about trying to figure out sound theory and sophisticated audio editing. I'll teach you some quick steps on how to use a free software called Audacity that will get the job done.

The modern infrastructures built around podcasting—from the free editing software to the websites that will host you—are built for folks without computer savvy. The business models, and profits of these companies often depend on it.

To get started, at least two of these hosting sites are free. Typically, the first 3-5 hours or so will be free on Podbean and SoundCloud. That's all the hours you'll need at first, so take advantage!

It's worth putting forth these efforts to get your podcast out there, because once you have a podcast on the air, no matter how you do it and no matter what a critic says, it's live.

A podcast puts us all on an even playing field. The podcast you created in your basement about your favorite comic book strip from the morning newspaper in your childhood will be right next to the most famous podcasts in the world.

The Joe Rogan Experience, Serial, and *Radiolab* will be in the same search engine of iTunes as you after you complete the steps I outline in this book. Podcasting is an egalitarian movement; it is truly merit-based. Once you get it up there, if it's good, it'll be seen, and it could be seen in droves. No one can take it from you.

It reminds me of why I'm such a huge fan of the U.S. Open in golf. I love it because it's open to every American. In theory, anyone can qualify at their local club if they're good enough; it's all merit-based.

With the U.S. Open and a podcast, no one gets popular because they "knew the right guy" or are more well-connected than someone else. That's what's beautiful about a podcast. Everyone's on the same playing field.

1. Flip on your computer.
2. Record it
3. Post it.

It boils down to three easy steps to learn. You don't even need a guest. Talk about whatever it is that makes you happy; discuss whatever it is that makes you unique. Share your voice with us.

If you nail it, you don't even need to edit it. If you truly don't care and you just want the message out there, record it with the built-in microphone on your laptop.

These are extreme circumstances, and I definitely don't encourage doing it that way, but the point is, the bare minimum for getting a podcast accepted by iTunes and into the world is incredibly low. You don't have to be tech-savvy or spend hundreds of dollars and hours doing it.

I wrote this book to encourage people that would normally look at technology as a hurdle, to change their mindset, and become a creative content creator.

Podcasts—when it's just you and the microphone—are so simple and beautiful. It's such an easy way to get your message out there. It's a way to touch people's lives and to talk to people in an intimate way that you would have never been able to reach before, all thanks to the times we live in. When you have a positive and optimistic viewpoint towards this stuff, it changes everything.

I have this perspective because when I graduated from college, there were massive layoffs and negative job growth in the field I chose (print journalism). I had days of doubt where I was discouraged and downright depressed that I wasn't born 30 years earlier when a newspaper reporter out of college could build a life by doing just that.

Then the real world slapped me in the face, and I woke up, embraced reality and the fast digital times we live in. In this new chapter of my life, I've fallen in love with the endless possibilities of this information age. I'm amazed by all the doors that became unlocked once I began mastering some basic technologies.

It wasn't that complicated to master them! I believe the cognitive overload that went on at that podcast workshop that I referenced earlier is happening way too much. We're over-teaching and overcomplicating things like podcasting.

Done is better than perfect. You have to just get something recorded, and get it out there. That's the first step. All good things happen after you've made the effort.

When it comes to podcasting, too many people are getting way too much information to the point where it discourages them. You do not have to be tech savvy to do this. I've fallen in love with podcasting, and I've written this book to teach in the simplest, fastest and cheapest way, how to get into iTunes, which is also known as "Apple Podcasts."

Truth be told, it doesn't matter what it's called. Just know there's an app on smart phones where you can get podcasts and because of its friendly algorithm (the way it ranks your podcast in the search engine), it's a golden opportunity for everyone with an itch to podcast.

People can find your content efficiently through this search engine. It makes it easier to get your message out to a larger audience. It's much faster than building a blog from scratch.

We're still at the beginning of this podcast tidal wave, and it's not going to stop. You have to get your messages out there now because the future is never certain. That algorithm that ranks podcasts in iTunes could change.

And a final note on why I love podcasting so much…

Well, it's something that can be done at night.

According to an episode of the legendary HBO sitcom, *Curb Your Enthusiasm*, Larry David (co-creator of *Seinfeld* and one of the greatest comedic writers and artists of all-time) once proposed a question:

"What can you really do at night?"

He uttered this with a gushing hint of cynicism/sarcasm in his voice.

He may have been right. I know that his point was all in jest, but there's always some serious truth in comedy.

Just like Larry suggests, you can go out and have dinner, sure. You can see a movie, or maybe do some karaoke, and of course, there is bowling. But that's essentially it!

(Okay. There are obviously a few other things you can do at night, but you get the point.)

I'm introducing the art of podcasting as a new activity to do with your friends at night.

That's right. Podcasting can be a social activity! It's so fun. Look at podcasting as a vehicle for increasing your happiness in life. That's the only expectation you should have for it.

For example, my best friend and I in Philadelphia get together and have dinner whenever I'm in town. Afterwards, we'll have a beer and then head up to his studio, which is really just a part of his house with a table, laptop and two chairs.

We plug in the microphone and talk college football; we're not masterminds of the game, but we both enjoy it. We sound off our opinions.

A few hours later, it's out there on iTunes, and the whole

world can hear from us. It's pretty unique, and it's actually some of the best memories we have as friends. We look forward to the next time I'm in Philly so we can get back to having another one of my guest appearances on his podcast.

We don't worry about mistakes. We just shoot from the hip. It's authentic, and our expectations are just to have fun and talk about what we both love - college football.

Podcasting is a liberating form of self- expression. It's therapeutic for me. Getting these thoughts off my chest and out into the world makes me happy. It's something everyone can easily be doing.

Everyone has a unique perspective, and everyone's story is different. Everyone is passionate about something in this life, and anyone can start a podcast.

Why not share that story with the world? Podcasting is the right medium to do it. Letting a little bit of discomfort with the technology and software stand in your way shouldn't be acceptable. Not with this medium. And that right there, is why I wrote this book.

CHAPTER 2
WHAT YOU NEED

When it comes to creating a podcast you need time. That doesn't mean you have to be retired or unemployed though, and it definitely doesn't mean you can't have kids. You just need a little bit of extra time, but way less time than you might think.

A common misconception about podcasting is that you need to update it regularly and forever. Some people think that once you start a podcast, you better keep feeding it. That might be true when it comes to a blog or even a social media account but not a podcast.

You don't want to start a blog or a social media account and then leave it empty as the years tick by. It looks sad when your latest post is six years ago, while the rest of your website is updated. Creating quality blog posts are tough, so that happens all the time.

The blog or social media account that the person just didn't have the time to keep feeding ends up looking bad. Outdated social media accounts and blogs with tumbleweeds of inactivity can reflect poorly on your overall brand and commitment.

No matter what you are trying to convey or share with the world. It screams "amateur hour," but a podcast is not the same.

You don't have to keep feeding a podcast. A podcast can have a lifespan. A podcast is much different. You can create a small series for a podcast (much like a miniseries on Netflix) with six episodes and then call it quits. Then that podcast is out there forever. Maybe one day a sound clip about that dog you rescued will go viral. You'll land on the *Today Show* and *Good Morning America.* Anything is possible once you've made the effort.

Remember that you don't have to keep feeding your podcast forever. You can create a few episodes of non-fiction or fiction just to test the waters. All you'll need is a little time to plan it out.

Create a list of bulleted points about what you want to say. Create an editorial calendar. An editorial calendar is your content plan. Create it by writing down what episode you want to do first, second, third, etc.

An editorial calendar isn't necessary, but it could give you some direction on what topics you plan to cover and when. (I've included an editorial calendar example in the Appendix at the end of this book.)

You can release your episodes all at once. Maybe you release a new episode once a week, once a month or even once a year. It's really just up to you.

I wouldn't recommend once a year (or even once a month). It's difficult to build a following that way, but it beats releasing them never.

If you can do it weekly, that's probably your best bet for building a following, but there are no real rules here. That's why I love it. Whatever you want to do is ultimately going to be fine. You just need time.

Speaking of time, a lot of people wonder how long a podcast needs to be. I get asked my opinion on how long each podcast episode should go for. My answer is always the same. Don't worry about it.

Don't let podcasting to a set time bother you unless your guest (should you choose to have one) is pressed for time.

If you make it sacrosanct to always have your podcast go for 30 minutes, you might work really hard to try to stretch, and stall or filibuster. All of this will result in a poorly made podcast. Your audience won't be fooled, and they'll smell the low-quality "filler" content from a mile away.

On the other hand, if you want to wrap everything up in 20 minutes and you have 40 minutes of quality content that needs to be covered, you're going to leave your audience disappointed. They're going to know.

Don't worry about length; make it as long as it needs to be. That's the beauty of podcasting. This isn't an episode of *Friends* or *The Office* where there's a set runtime that you need to fill for advertisers and network scheduling.

This is free-form art and expression, and it can be as a long as you want. It can also be as a short as you want it to be. I've released a two-minute podcast before on iTunes. It's not an issue.

On the opposite end of the spectrum there are episodes of the *Joe Rogan Experience* podcast that go for more than four hours. If it's quality podcasting, let it keep going.

Just get it recorded and put it out there to the world.

Computer

You need a computer to get a podcast done in the most efficient way possible. You'll be able to record and edit your audio directly with it. A laptop works best since its portable. You will also need a microphone.

USB Microphone

I recommend a USB microphone. They call it a USB microphone because it can easily and directly be plugged into the USB port which is standard on just about any computer made since the Backstreet Boy's heyday.

I got my USB microphone from Amazon. One microphone is good enough.

I use an **Audio-Technica AT2020** (about $150 on Amazon) and it connects directly to the USB port in my laptop, but you don't even need anything that fancy. You can work your way up to that later.

A Blue Snowball USB Microphone (about $50 on Amazon) is a happy medium. It's great quality and will help you get exactly what you need.

You could technically just record your voice directly into your computer's internal microphone. If all you want to do is get the podcast out there. However, I don't recommend doing that because it wouldn't sound right. It'd be too annoyingly muffled for an audience to enjoy it, but technically you *could* do it.

At the very least, you should pick up the cheapest USB microphone you can find. Just type "cheap USB microphone" into a Google search, and you'll be able to find one that sells for about $20. Walmart.com has some low prices on USB microphones too.

I can't vouch for the quality of the super cheap USB microphones, but read some reviews on Amazon if you're skeptical. The point is, don't worry about it being perfect; just get it recorded.

Audacity

Next, you need to download Audacity. Audacity is where you will record and eventually edit your podcast. It is completely free.

Visit https://www.audacityteam.org/download/ to get it. (Please note that the hyperlinks in this book are always subject to change, and thoroughly searching Google is a nice workaround if any of these links have expired.)

After you think Audacity has successfully installed, you may want to restart your computer, just to cover all of your bases. Audacity will be a key factor in this podcast creation process, so it's vitally important that either you or a loved one figures out how to download and install it. Just follow all the prompts and you'll be good.

I believe it is easier to figure out how to record and edit a podcast as a beginner by using the Windows operating system (which comes standard with almost every computer these days that isn't made by Apple). Most of my instructions are meant for users of Windows.

If you have a Mac, that doesn't mean game over. Either operating system will get the job done. Audacity is readily available to download for both Mac and Windows.

There are plenty of Audacity tutorial YouTube videos out there depending on how bad you want to master it. You don't need to fall into a YouTube rabbit hole to understand the basics of Audacity that will lead to a finished podcast though.

The main thing to remember is that once your USB microphone is plugged in, you must select your USB microphone in the drop-down menu next to the microphone icon in Audacity before you hit record. If everything is plugged in correctly and you don't see your microphone, close Audacity and restart it.

Once you have Audacity open, somewhere near the top-left corner of Audacity will be a tiny microphone icon. To the right of that icon will be a drop-down menu. This is where you will select the USB microphone you've already plugged in.

For example, the name of my microphone is the Audio-Technica AT2020. When I click on this drop-down menu, one of my options appears as *Microphone (AT2020 USB)*. This is the option I select. If Audacity isn't finding your microphone, double-check to make sure it's plugged in properly and there are no loose connections. If you have multiple USB ports on your computer, try a different port.

Let's recap where you should be at now.

1. You've downloaded Audacity and opened it up.
2. You've plugged in your USB microphone.
3. You've selected that USB microphone in Audacity's microphone drop-down menu.
4. Hit record (the big red circle) in Audacity.
5. Talk into your microphone!

That's right. Hit record in Audacity and the magic is made. You are making art now. It's that fast and that simple. You don't have to worry about all the extra bells and whistles in Audacity right now.

Turn the air conditioner off to make sure the ambient noises in the room are kept to a minimum, and/or learn how to use Audacity's Noise Reduction tool in post-production later (there are endless YouTube videos on this stuff), it's your choice! I've included instructions on how to use Audacity's Noise Reduction tool in the Appendix at the end of this book.

If the dog barks in the middle of your monologue, introduce Fido. It's best to be real on a podcast. Crack a joke about it. Laugh.

Just plug-in and start talking about your subject matter. That's it. You did it. You just made magic, and all it took was some knowledge on how to download Audacity for free and buying a $22 USB microphone from Walmart.com. You're so close to being in the official podcast club now.

Even if you went super cheap on a microphone, as long as it doesn't sound like complete muffled garbage and you're not bumping into it, the odds are in favor of it being good enough!

This is your first podcast. You're getting experience. You're learning what you like about the equipment. You're learning about Audacity just by playing with some of the buttons.

You're getting experience through repetition, through physically doing it. Don't sit back and read a bunch of things on the Internet all day after you've downloaded Audacity.

I showed you how to find your microphone, now practice recording your voice in Audacity. It's all about building that muscle memory in your brain and getting a little more comfortable with it each time. Keep at it.

If you aren't very tech savvy to begin with, I would recommend staying away from portable digital audio recorders. A computer with Audacity will be much simpler for you.

If your podcast involves you needing to walk around while you record it, use a smartphone and convert the audio to an MP3 later, or if you insist, take the time to learn how to use a portable digital audio recorder with an attached microphone. It's not beginner-level stuff, but it's far from rocket science.

Watch YouTube videos, Google it thoroughly and talk to the folks in person at the brick and mortar stores that carry this product to learn it from all angles. You have to be resourceful if you want to be a "roving reporter" while you podcast. As always, it comes back to your will and how bad you want it.

A portable digital audio recorder, such as the very popular Zoom Handy Recorder, converts audio into digital form. You won't need to use this unless you want to be moving around a lot while you're recording the podcast. An example of this would be recording a podcast about colonial mansions in Williamsburg and needing to walk around the mansion with a tour guide to talk about everything you encounter during the podcast.

Talk about a very specific and thought-provoking podcast! However, this is probably not something you're going to need to do as a beginner.

I recommend trying to avoid this option if you are a podcaster who is just starting out. If logistically, you can get by on recording directly into Audacity on a computer with the USB microphone, you'll be good.

With the combination of Audacity and a USB microphone, your sound quality will be just as strong as if you were to use a Zoom microphone. In addition, it will save you the steps of then having to transfer the audio from your Zoom microphone onto your computer to edit it.

Don't get lost in the details about what you need. Make it easy on yourself as you start out. Just have a computer and record directly into Audacity. If you have a guest, get the microphone placed between you and the guest while it's plugged into the computer and record it into Audacity. Keep your voice loud and firm. It doesn't take any sort of tech savvy to speak loud and clear! Don't shout though.

Once you've downloaded Audacity, you don't even need Wi-Fi or an internet connection during your interview. You just need some strong battery life in that computer (or make sure it's plugged into an outlet).

Please note that you will need a reliable internet connection if you want to record a podcast with someone in a different location than you. I'll discuss that later when we talk about using Skype to record interviews with folks in different locations.

LAME MP3 Encoder

There is something called a LAME MP3 Encoder that you need to download. It will allow you to create an MP3 file from your recording inside Audacity. If you can download Audacity, you can download this Encoder. It's free too. It's just one extra step you have to do to get your coveted MP3 file (the ticket to Podcast glory).

When you finish recording, you'll "Export" your work in Audacity as an MP3 file, and save it to your computer. In order for Audacity to accomplish this simple task, you'll need one more piece of free software and that's the "Lame MP3 Encoder."

This encoder, which operates unseen in the background, will allow Audacity to export your work as an MP3. This is the file type that you will be submitting your podcast to iTunes with later on.

You can try finding the Lame MP3 Encoder here:

https://lame.buanzo.org/#lamewindl

[And click on the link that says *RECOMMENDED Installer Package for Windows*.]

Of course, that link is subject to change, but it could give you an idea of what you should be looking for.

If you're on a Mac, it's going to take a little more digging.

Google search, "Lame MP3 Encoder for Audacity Mac User" and then download and install it on your computer.

It's simply a matter of downloading free software and patiently waiting for it to install on your computer. If you really can't figure it out, ask someone you trust with computers and technology. They will be able to help you if you can describe to them exactly what you need. We all know that tech-savvy person in our life, maybe it's a youngster who you've spoiled on countless birthdays over the years. Now it's time to call in some favors!

After you've successfully downloaded the Encoder, you will export the Audacity recording into an MP3 file. To do this, open Audacity.

At the very top left portion of Audacity, there will be a menu bar. The first option should be called *File*. Click on *File* and a drop-down menu will appear below *File*. One of the options will be called *Export Audio*. Click on *Export Audio*.

After you've done that, an *Export Audio* box will appear.

To the right of where it says *File name:* you will name the recording, and to the right of where it says *Save as type* you will select *MP3 Files* from the list of options, and then click the *Save* button. (Ignore the *Edit Meta Data* box that opens next; don't enter any data, just click the *OK* button).

Save the MP3 file somewhere on your computer where you can easily find it later, such as your computer's desktop.

Headphones

People always ask if they need the fancy/expensive noise-cancelling headphones. No. You don't need headphones at all. Make it simple for yourself. Have the microphone plugged in and talk into it with your guest. Headphones are not necessary.

(You'll need a cheap pair of earbud headphones if you want

to record podcast interviews remotely with Skype, but we'll discuss that later.)

If you're just starting out and your goal is to get a podcast out there, because your content is great, have that USB microphone plugged in and hold it between you and the guest. Or set the microphone stand between you and the guest. Speak loud and clear. You'll be good. No headphones needed.

You definitely don't need headphones if you are doing a monologue podcast either.

In fact, that $22 USB microphone you just bought probably has a little stand with it. Sit on one side of the microphone and have your other guest sit on the other side and talk. Have a conversation. This way isn't awkward, trust me. I've podcasted millions of times with one microphone. It works.

People love to be interviewed. They're not going to think twice that you only have one microphone.

Windscreen

It's not a terrible idea to buy a windscreen or a pop filter for the microphone (if it doesn't already come with it); this will help stop any of the "popping sounds" from damaging your smooth audio tracks.

A "popping p" is the most common "popping noise" that has the tendency for an audio track to briefly sound like you are recording in a wind tunnel. It can be avoided by carefully articulating words, though a windscreen on the microphone can also help. These aren't necessary though. So, if it poses a problem, I suggest cutting this step out until you become a more advanced podcaster.

I'd like to reiterate on carefully articulating words. Your voice is clearly a massively important part of a podcast. Invest some time in learning about breathing exercises and other tips you can incorporate to improve your chances of sounding like a pro. YouTube is all you need for this, and it's free.

Let's review this one more time. So, if you have a guest in-person, just have them come into your living room (or a relatively quiet and enclosed space) and have them talk in the microphone with you. It's that straightforward! You don't need a studio or super nice headphones to podcast.

Skype

Say you want to have someone call into your podcast because you live in Cleveland and they live in Seattle. OK, now you're up for a little-advanced lesson, but relax, it's easy and if your guest knows how to Skype, it's free.

Skype is a telephone system that works by direct communication between users' computers on the Internet, without the need for a central server.

Skype is free. You should be using Skype. In fact, the first step towards having someone call into your podcast is downloading Skype.

You can also use Google Hangouts (also free) to record a guest from across the world, but I recommend Skype.

There are two key steps to recording a remote podcast:

1. Have your guest call you on Skype.
2. Record the sounds coming from your computer (don't hold a microphone up to your computer speakers to do this, you'll get far better quality via the reliable and free software trick that I'm about to teach you).

Using Skype and recording the sounds coming from your computer are crucial skills to learn. From a logistical standpoint, your podcast will be able to get so many more guests as they can simply call in to your show. Think of all the savings in travel this will add up to!

Now let's go to work. You've already got Skype, which you can download for free but now you need something to record your computer sounds with.

To do this, you will download free software called VoiceMeeter. Guess what? VoiceMeeter is free too!

That's right. Everything I've so far told you about, other than the computer (that you probably already own) and the USB microphone is free.

VoiceMeeter

You can download VoiceMeeter here:

https://www.vb-audio.com/Voicemeeter/

VoiceMeeter is called donationware because if you have a little extra money on hand, you can donate to VoiceMeeter. It helps the developers, and it helps the software stay updated, but if you don't have the money, it's totally okay. It is still free.

After it downloads and installs, open VoiceMeeter.

By the way, you should have Skype, Audacity and VoiceMeeter all open now.

Before your guest calls you on Skype, make sure to set "VoiceMeeter Input" as your Playback device. Do this on Windows by right-clicking on the speaker icon that should be at the bottom right-hand corner of your screen.

In many common versions of the Windows operating system, such as Windows 10, it will appear to the left of where the time of day and date appear in the far right-hand corner of your screen. The icon should look like this:

You will right-click on this speaker icon. After you right-click on the speaker icon, a menu should then appear in front of the speaker icon. One of the options will be called *Sounds*. Left-click on *Sounds*.

After clicking on *Sounds*, a box will open with different tabs and options. Inside this box, you will left-click on the tab that is labeled *Playback*.

There should be some language that says *Select a playback device below to modify its settings:*

One of the devices as an option should be called *VoiceMeeter Input*. Click on the *VoiceMeeter Input* option, and then click on the button that says *Set Default*. A green checkmark should appear next to the *VoiceMeeter Input* option now.

Next you will click on the *OK* button.

After clicking the *OK* button, you will open up VoiceMeeter. Near the top-left corner of VoiceMeeter, you should see a large number 1 with the words *HARDWARE INPUT* appearing to the right of the large number 1.

Click on the Number 1 and a drop-down menu should appear below it. If it's plugged into your computer, your USB microphone should appear as one of the options to select in this drop-down menu. Make sure the USB microphone that you want to record with is selected.

Next, open up Audacity. In the top-left portion of Audacity's screen, you will see the microphone icon that we talked about earlier. Click on the drop-down menu that appears to the right of this microphone icon and select *VoiceMeeter Output* as your microphone.

Have your guest call you on Skype, and hit the giant red record button in Audacity to test this all out. Audacity should be recording both you (because you're speaking into your microphone) and your guest (because it's recording the sounds coming from your computer).

One final step is to make sure Skype is picking up your USB microphone as its default microphone.

Open Skype and sign in. There should be three dots at the top of Skype's menu. When you hover your cursor over the three dots a box should appear that says *More*. Click on these three dots and a menu of options called *Settings* should appear.

One of the options within Settings should be called *Audio & Video*. Click on *Audio & Video*. Make sure the *Microphone* in this portion of Skype's Settings is set to the USB microphone that you should already have plugged in.

Earbud Headphones

Earbud headphones are cheap and widely available. If you don't have any lying around the house (they've been coming free with iPhones since 2007 or so), pick up a cheap pair on Amazon.

Plug your earbuds into the jack of your computer or speakers. I recommend that you leave one earbud in your ear, and one out. This lets you hear your caller on Skype and allows you to hear yourself talk at the same time.

You don't need to have the video turned on when you use Skype. Call your guest using an "Audio Call" in Skype as video is not necessary for podcasts. This makes it easier. Sometimes people don't want to be seen, maybe their hair or makeup isn't done; just make it easier for everyone and tell them upfront that it's going to be an audio-only call.

Skype Number

Your guest might not know how to use Skype. This is a common issue that you might face. Not everyone uses it. And unlike you, not everyone is open-minded to investing a couple minutes and some clicks to figure it out.

In America, and dozens of other countries, you can buy a Skype phone number as a workaround! Amazing how another barrier has been lifted!

A Skype number costs roughly $55 to own for one year, but it could save you $55,000 worth of headaches. With the purchase of a Skype number, you will get a local phone number that you own. With this number, your guests will be able to call you from anywhere in the world on a landline or cell phone.

This lifts another huge hurdle because your guest won't even have to know how to use Skype. They'll just have to dial the number you bought. Yes, it costs a few bucks, but if you're serious about podcasting with guests around the globe, it may be time to tighten your belt and buy a Skype number.

There is a lot of highly expensive telecommunications equipment that can cost hundreds (and thousands) of dollars in order to record phone calls for a podcast. I'm here to say you don't need it.

The only expense you may want to consider here is a Skype number (and that's only if you're certain your guests won't know how to use Skype).

When I first started podcasting, I didn't buy the Skype number. I just assumed people knew how to use Skype, and at first it was fine because my guests did in fact know how to use it. Then we expanded our podcast, and there were guests that did not know how to use Skype.

Rather than waste time trying to train them on how to use Skype, I just bought a Skype number and now they call me, and we can record interviews all over the world. Get a feel for your audience at first. Don't buy a Skype number until it's time you know you must.

The latest link available to buy a Skype number is here:

https://www.skype.com/en/features/online-number/

You'll be able to nab a Skype number if you have a free Skype account and live in a country where Skype numbers are available. As of this book's publishing, online Skype numbers are available in the following countries:

- Australia
- Brazil
- Chile
- Denmark
- Estonia
- Finland
- France
- Hong Kong
- Hungary
- Ireland
- Japan
- Korea
- Malta
- Mexico
- Netherlands
- New Zealand
- Poland
- Romania
- South Africa
- Sweden

- Switzerland
- United States
- United Kingdom

If a Skye number isn't an option for where you live, don't worry. You'll just have to make sure the other person that you are interviewing knows how to use Skype in the traditional way. Look at a Skype number as a pure luxury.

Now, let's talk about my favorite aspect of podcasting - the interview process.

CHAPTER 3
THE INTERVIEW

I like to set an editorial calendar in advance before I launch a new podcast series. It's a way to map out what episodes you want to release and when, but you don't have to get this strategic. After all, *this is an art*. You can dive right into it.

Things are most simple if you just want to do a monologue and not have a guest. You'll flip on Audacity, plug in your USB microphone and hit record. Talk to the world about what you want to talk about.

You should prepare for your monologue though. Create a bulleted list of topics that you want to cover during your podcast, but do not write it out verbatim. Never write out a podcast word for word, it sounds bad. It doesn't sound authentic and this medium thrives on authenticity.

If you write something out word for word and you start

reading it; it's an audio book, it's not really a podcast. Odds are you don't have the sweet, soothing voice of one of those audio book voice-over artists either, so, it'll just sound like a bad audio book. Again, people aren't mentally preparing to listen to an audio book, they're mentally preparing for a podcast which is much more informal and freeform.

Just bullet out topics that you want to talk about, and then speak freely on those topics. Remember that it's not live so don't worry about saying something stupid. You can just go back and edit it later which is easy and which we'll talk about later.

If you want to check out a hilarious monologue-style podcast, I recommend Bill Burr's the *Monday Morning Podcast*. There are plenty of great monologue podcasts out there to listen to if you want to get inspired.

If you want to go the more traditional route and have an interview subject on your program, that's cool too. Just make sure to bullet out a list of topics or questions that you want to discuss with your guest(s) before the interview. Email these topics or questions to your interview subject beforehand.

Invite your guest on the program in an email similar to this template:

SUBJECT of email: **Podcast Interview Request**

Dear Guest,

I hope all is well. I'm pleased to announce I'm launching a podcast soon about XYZ. I was hoping we could get together to record an interview.

I know you'll be a great expert for us on this podcast. Attached to this email is a brief outline of some of the questions we'll discuss, and some talking points for you to consider. The podcast will be 100% audio, and it's not live so we can go back and re-record items if we want. The interview should take about X minutes or so.

Please take a look at the outline when you get a chance and let me know if you can assist. Thanks so much for your consideration, and if you can't find the time, I totally understand and want to thank you anyways!

Sincerely,
Your Name

Here is an example of the podcast outline you will attach to your podcast request email:

Podcast Outline
Interview with Guest XYZ

Opening Remarks

Host will ask the guest to introduce him or herself and tell the audience about their work.

Interview/Discussion

1. Topic or Question to discuss No. 1
2. Topic or Question to discuss No. 2
3. Topic or Question to discuss No. 3
4. Do you have any final thoughts before we end the interview?

Closing Remarks
- Thank audience and guest/co-host
- For more information, please visit: the guest's website, twitter handle, etc.

The point is that you want to send this list of proposed topics to keep you and your guest on track. Sometimes, when you get off a topic, it's OK and it sounds real. Podcasts are all about exploring unchartered territory, but your guest might not have all the time in the world.

Best practice is to find out if your guest is under a time constraint before you record.

Out of respect for your guest's time, you may want to create a list of the most important points that you plan to cover in your interview. Make sure there is an informal checklist of topics or questions to cover in front of you when you record.

The list of proposed topics can help put them at ease a little bit. Having a more relaxed guest typically results in a better conversation.

Let them know you respect their complete commitment to your podcast, but you kindly request they do not write out their answers or talking points word for word. If you notice them doing that during the recording, you should kindly nudge them in the other direction.

Let them know they don't have to go over things verbatim, and they can just speak freely about the topics.

If that doesn't work, try saying something such as, "I want to go off script for a minute, are you okay with that?" And then ask a new question. That will hopefully get them to be a little less stiff and rigid.

You have to be a quarterback who can call an audible. You have to be able to think on your feet a little bit as a podcaster. You have to always be listening during the interview, and at the same time thinking about your next question.

Listening is the most important skill. Yes, you have to be able to call an audible and go off topic once in a while, but listening is the most important key to unlocking a great conversation.

That's why you prepare and create lists beforehand. You're going to be listening and not thinking deeply about things to say during an interview. Glance down at your list from time to time and cross items out after you've covered them.

You can't be thinking too much about what you're going to say next. You'll get caught off guard and accidently repeat yourself; awkward interviews are inevitable if you're not listening.

Listen intently and when the person stops talking, look down at your notes and make sure you cover the next topic until all items have been discussed.

Before the interview, you might want to calm your guest down a bit. Try putting them in a state of Zen. Let them know if they misspeak, you'll be able to back up the recording and you can re-record it.

Put them at ease. Let them know this isn't live, they're not going to be on video and they don't need to worry about their hair or makeup.

At the Podcast Movement Conference I attended, Terry Gross the legendary interviewer from NPR's *Fresh Air* was a keynote speaker. Terry is widely considered one of the best interviewers of our time.

She shared a story with us that stuck with me. She talked about interviewing George Clooney in 2005. He discussed a painful injury he incurred while shooting a scene in one of his newest movies.

When Terry asked him about it, Clooney spoke honestly about the pain. He even mentioned thoughts of suicide that had crept into his mind. Terry said these comments were taken out of context by some major media outlets and it ended up doing Clooney quite a disservice from a public relations standpoint.

Clooney was completely open and honest. It was a jarring reminder of how interview guests are putting themselves in very vulnerable spots when they agree to be interviewed by you.

Terry reiterated that you have to remember people are taking a lot of risks when they choose to be interviewed by you. When folks are open and honest, she stressed the need to have empathy in your heart during the interview.

This is true in the medium of podcasts especially. Discussions can get deeply emotional and revealing.

When all is said and done, 99% of what you are focusing on is listening. Even when it's boring... you have to keep listening! You don't want to get caught napping and look foolish.

You should always find out how to pronounce the full name of your interview subject. If it's impossible to find out (which I suppose could happen), open the interview off and just say something along the lines of:

Hello and welcome to our podcast, I'm going to let our guest introduce himself (or herself) right now.

Most of all, during an interview, you have to be authentic.

Being yourself is the number one way to make your podcast interesting and to have it stand out from the pack.

When it comes to new media and the infinite amount of content being created, the way to step out and to be different is to be you.

The only truly unique thing you bring to the table is yourself, and don't underestimate how much that means.

Be real, be authentic. People have seen it all in this Internet age, and it has probably already been done, but it hasn't been done by you in your style. When you're confident about being yourself, you create a unique identity.

If you're a curious person by nature, you have a huge advantage.

Whatever questions pop into your head are probably going to work. Feed those questions to your guest and get them out there, even if it's random (if it truly doesn't work, you can delete it later). Your authenticity is the number one value you bring to the podcasting world.

The beauty of what you're doing right now is recording everything in Audacity. It's going to help your workflow in the near future, because Audacity is the same software that you're going to use to edit your podcast.

You get to record and edit your podcast in the same software. Audacity is quite phenomenal!

CHAPTER 4
EDITING AND POSTING YOUR PODCAST

After recording the entire podcast in Audacity, you'll continue using our old friend Audacity to edit it.

When your recording is done in Audacity, hit the big red stop button at the top of the screen; it's the circle with a red square in it, that sits next to the play button. (Please note that your version of Audacity may not look exactly like what I am describing. You may have a more updated version of Audacity, but everything will still essentially look and work the same.)

You will also select the little icon that looks like an "I". This "I" icon is located to the right of the record button at the top-right portion of Audacity. It is called the Selection

Tool. It sits next to the magnifying glass icon (which will be discussing later).

Move your cursor to the beginning of the recording with the "I" shaped Selection Tool. You may need to use the scroll bar at the bottom of the screen as well to get your cursor to the very beginning of the audio track.

The scroll bar appears above where it says *Project Rate (HZ)*. You'll only need to know how to scroll from left to right with this scroll bar so you can get back to the beginning of your audio track and listen to it.

[Things like *Project Rate (HZ)* are completely unnecessary for you to understand in Audacity. There are so many bells and whistles in Audacity, and it can overwhelm you. If you're a beginner, it's best to simply ignore just about everything in Audacity that I don't mention explicitly in this book.]

Hit the play button so you can start listening.

Listen carefully to your audio. When there's an "um" or "ya know" (filler words), those can be taken out. Take out things like coughs too.

You can tell exactly what waves of audio you want to take out because it will be obvious when you listen to it and look at the wave form of audio at the same time.

Highlight the waves of audio that you want gone by clicking and dragging the cursor over it, and then hit the delete key on your keyboard. If you want it back, navigate to the *Edit* menu option (to the right of *File*) and then click

Undo. (*Undo* should be the first option in the *Edit* drop-down menu).

It's not necessary to get rid of every single filler word, but too many "ums" can be harsh on the ears.

The other cursor you should become familiar with in Audacity (besides the "I" Selection Tool) is the magnifying glass. You'll have to know how to zoom in and out on the audio's wave form with this magnifying glass icon. It is called the Zoom Tool.

This magnifying glass Zoom Tool will allow you to make more precise selections of the exact pieces of audio that you want to cut. The magnifying glass is located next to the "I" Selection Tool.

To zoom in on the audio wave form, click the magnifying glass icon at the top of Audacity to make sure it's selected. Then move the cursor over the wave of audio you want to zoom in on and left-click on your mouse. To zoom out, simply right-click on your mouse.

Just remember when you are using the magnifying glass Zoom Tool that you have to re-select the "I" shaped Selection Tool before you can select the audio wave form to copy, paste or delete it.

When you think you're done, save that track as an MP3 file, by navigating to *File* at the top of Audacity, and select *Export Audio* from the drop-down menu items.

Name your file next to where it says *File name:* and select the *Save as type* as *MP3 files* (*MP3 files* will appear in the drop-down menu under *Save as type*).

Click the *Save* button. (ignore the *Edit Meta Data* box that opens next, don't enter any data, and then click the *OK* button). NOTE: As long as you've already downloaded the LAME MP3 Encoder, like we discussed in Chapter 2, this will work.

If you want to add some additional audio to your podcast episode later, you can do that in Audacity as well.

For example, as part of his wildly popular podcast, comedian Marc Maron will talk at length about whatever is on his mind before he introduces an audio track of the interview with him and his guest.

He pre-records this monologue at a different time from when he interviews his guest. He (or whoever edits his podcast) will then combine the two separate MP3 files into one combined track for his listeners.

To add additional audio to your podcast:

1. Record a new track of whatever you want to say in Audacity, and export it as an MP3 file (save it to where you can easily find it).
2. Re-open the original Audacity project where you want to add your new recording.
3. Add the new recording in Audacity by navigating to the menu at the top clicking *File>Import Audio*.
4. Navigate to where you saved your new MP3 file to add and import it into Audacity.

Your new audio will appear as a separate track below the

original recording in Audacity. That's okay because you can copy and paste wave forms of audio wherever you want, just like you can copy and paste text in a Microsoft Word document wherever you want.

Get in the habit of re-listening carefully to the recording each time after you delete, copy, and paste audio to make sure it all flows and makes sense.

When you export the final product from Audacity into an MP3 file (like we discussed earlier), Audacity will combine all tracks into one for your eventual listener.

There are hundreds of YouTube videos available to watch about how to use Audacity. Look for the videos with hundreds of thousands (if not millions) of views. Those are typically the best, but you don't have to be an expert.

Don't get overwhelmed though with instructions on how to edit audio, slowly keep learning more and more by using Audacity more and more. Practice on.

Once you're familiar with Audacity, you can do anything in the podcast world.

Did you take out all those "ums" and filler words? Did you take out that piece of audio in the middle of the recording where you're coaching the guest? If you recorded yourself saying a thing to your guest like, "Do you want me to take that part out?" MAKE SURE IT GETS DELETED from the final version.

Please note that I've included instructions on how to use Audacity's Noise Reduction tool in the Appendix at the end of this book. The Noise Reduction tool is relatively simple to use and can take out annoying ambient sounds in the room (such as noisy HVAC equipment). It will provide you with one of the most powerful, simple (and free) post-production tools in the podcast universe.

After you've taken out the stuff in your podcast that you don't want, listen to it in its entirety one last time. Make sure you didn't leave anything in there by accident.

If you want to be a big shot, or if you're an uncompromising perfectionist, you can actually hire people on freelance services such as Fiverr.com or Upwork.com to do it for you. (I don't get paid by any of these services that I recommend. I mention them because they are the easiest way to get your stuff out there in the most affordable manner.)

Enter "Edit my podcast" within the search bar on Fiverr.com. There should be gigs starting at $5 or so for someone to edit your podcast. Although the site is called "fiverr", keep in mind that things can get considerably more expensive than $5.

Make sure to use freelancers that have a lot of reviews and high ratings.

This book is all about getting your podcast done. If you really want to have your podcast edited by a professional, it's unnecessary, but you can try it if you think it helps you get things done faster than doing it yourself.

You can pretty much get someone to do anything that you feel uncomfortable with on Fiverr.com.

In fact, if there is something in this entire process that you really don't want to do, or can't figure out, you can almost certainly get someone to work with you from Fiverr.com on it.

The substance of your podcast comes from you; you have to be able to interview people or speak at length about something you're passionate about.

If you rely too much on websites like Fiverr or Upwork, you risk losing the beauty of what makes the podcast unique (which is you). You're going to lose that authenticity if you rely a great deal on freelance labor.

Once you have the interview done, edited and it sounds right from start to finish, you might want to add some "bumper music" to the beginning and end of the podcast. This will help make it sound professional, but remember it's not so necessary to have this if you truly don't want to learn this step.

Bumper music is also known as theme music.

Bill Burr's *Monday Morning Podcast*, which is one of the most downloaded podcasts in the world, does not have any introduction or bumper music. Bill just hits record and starts talking.

Bill is one of the most successful comedians of our time, so he can also pretty much do whatever he wants, and people will still tune in. With that in mind, I do recommend adding bumper music to your podcast. You can have the music slowly fade in at the beginning, and then have it slowly fade out at the end. This can spice up your podcast.

Don't have music play in the background of your podcast for its entire duration. That's a bit much, but bumper music at the beginning and end of your show should work great.

It's important to get in the habit of importing MP3 audio files into Audacity because that is how you will add new audio to your projects, including bumper music.

You'll need to have the music that you want to add as bumper music in an MP3 file readily available. Just make sure you have the rights to use the music!

You will add that music as a second track below the track of your recording (Audacity will automatically do this for you when you import the MP3 file containing your bumper music).

To fade music in or out, click your mouse and drag the Selection Tool over the audio track of the music that you want to modify in Audacity. Next, on the Audacity toolbar at the top of the page, you can select the *Effect* drop-down menu. Select the *Fade In* and *Fade Out* features on the *Effect* drop-down menu to get the music just right.

You can also lower the volume of the bumper music by highlighting the music with the Selection Tool, and then navigating to *Effect* as part of Audacity's top menu items. One of the menu items appearing underneath *Effect* will be called *Amplify*. Click on *Amplify* and a box should open up.

Inside this box is where you will modify each track's volume with the blue slider bar. You can turn up the volume of a track of audio you've selected and you can turn it down as well. Click the *OK* button after you've modified the audio, and re-listen to it to see how it came out. You can always use the *Undo* option underneath *Edit* if you dislike the end result.

There are a lot of legal aspects involved with music licensing that you will need to know about. This will help you avoid legal issues. It will also prevent your podcast from being taken down. You have to play by the rules when you add music.

Yes, we would all love to add the latest Maroon 5 jam on our podcast to start it off, but you have to be realistic. These people are artists too. If you cannot afford to pay them; you cannot use their music. The good news is that there are plenty of websites that offer you affordable stock music.

For those without a marketing background, essentially the term "stock" means it's professionally done and is available to buy the rights to use.

Be very careful though. A lot of the licenses that come with stock music stipulate that you do not use the music more than once. A lot of the license agreements are for one-time use only.

Try to avoid using the websites that offer single-use licenses. It'll get costly. If you're looking for a website where you can buy it once and use it forever, I highly recommend a website called MusicBakery.com.

Again, I'm not getting paid by anyone to recommend any

of the software or websites that I mention. I use MusicBakery.com because you can buy it once and use it forever. They keep it simple; your music purchase includes a royalty free buyout license.

Now all of this is subject to change, but I really liked my experience with MusicBakery.com because I was able to reach a real person when I called their customer service phone number. Sometimes, you just want to speak to a person to have your questions about the license agreement (or anything) answered.

In the age we live, it's increasingly rare to land an actual person to speak with on the phone when it comes to customer service; the fine folks at MusicBakery.com answered all my questions when I called them.

I want to issue a fair warning that many of the other software and websites that you use to launch your podcasts will not have customer service centers where you can get your questions answered.

They do this to save money, but the good news is there are large communities of support out there through YouTube, message boards, etc. With so much crowdsourcing going on, odds are that someone has already proposed your exact question to a reliable message board and your answer will await you there.

There's been so many times that I'll use websites to buy music only to learn that you have to keep buying the song every other time you use it. That means every single podcast episode may cost you $25 to use the song, but with MusicBakery.com you pay maybe 40-50 dollars, and you can use that song forever.

While I don't recommend it, you could use Google to try and find a free track you can use. The quality probably won't be great, but if it's free, it's free.

You have to read things thoroughly to make sure it's indeed free though, because sometimes what looks free will not be free.

If you buy a track to use from a website such as MusicBakery.com, they will give you the MP3 file to download with your purchase. You will then insert it into the beginning and/or end of your podcast using Audacity.

This will give you some professional sounding bumper music. In Audacity, you will import the new audio file you just bought and make it a little lower than the audio of you talking. Just let it play for a little bit before the first person starts talking on the podcast. It's a relatively simple way to give a splash of professionalism to your podcast.

I honestly think it's worth it. But remember, you don't have to have bumper music to get accepted as a podcast in iTunes/Apple Podcasts. Music simply adds a nice, professional touch.

If you have friends that are musicians, or if you're a musician yourself, create an original song. It's always best to use music that you own. The thing I love about MusicBakery.com is that you own it outright. With other popular sites, you typically are buying the song to use once. Those costs can add up.

I can't overemphasize it. If you don't read the music agreement license carefully, then you could put yourself in a very vulnerable position. Music is great, but it's not necessary. Again, if you want the most hassle-free experience, make sure you buy the song with a license to use it forever.

A lot of people bring up questions about using music and a legal term called Fair Use, claiming Fair Use could land you in court. Try to avoid it at all costs; using short clips of music won't help you either.

I've learned from lawyers at breakout sessions of the Podcast Movement Conference that the following is unfortunately true for podcasters:

- You can still get sued and have your podcast taken down even if you use just a little bit of the copyrighted song.
- It doesn't matter if you're non-profit or not making any money off it.

It won't matter if you are using the music for even just a split-second, you'll be putting yourself at risk of getting sued or getting your podcast taken down. It's not worth the risk in my view.

Some are surprised to learn lawyers and those seeking to protect musicians do not care if you are non-profit. I encourage everyone to create some social good with their podcast, but that still won't protect you. In the eyes of the law, it doesn't matter if you aren't making money when you use music illegally, your podcast will still get taken down.

Everyone is fair game here.

After you've added the music to your podcast, and you've listened to it thoroughly, you're ready for the final step. It's time to get that bad boy into iTunes, also called Apple Podcasts.

SoundCloud

Go to SoundCloud.com and sign up for a free account. You can also use Podbean.com and sign up for a free account. I like these two services because they traditionally will give you anywhere from 3-5 hours of audio completely free to host upfront. These services will also give you an RSS feed that you copy/paste into Apple Podcasts/iTunes later (the final step in getting your podcast official).

Besides SoundCloud and Podbean, there are other services you can use to host your podcast, including Blubrry and Libsyn.

Let's say you use SoundCloud. First, you will need a podcast title and image. What's the name of your podcast? That's easy; don't think too much about it.

Make up a title for it that's friendly to the iTunes search engine. Think about what people who want to hear your podcast will be searching for. What will people search for when they want to hear about subject matter similar to your podcast?

For example, if your podcast is about comedy clubs that you love to visit around the world, call it The *Comedy Club*

Traveler's Guide, or something like that.

A Tourist's Guide to Comedy Clubs could work too. Think about what people who are interested in comedy (or as I affectionately call them "comedy nerds") are going to be searching for.

Comedy would be a major keyword in this example, and certainly, a keyword related to travel should be in your podcast's title too.

Don't overthink it. Simply make a title and move on.

Your podcast needs a description. It's not rocket science. Have a description of what your podcast is about. Don't spend all day writing it. Just tell them what it's about. A couple of sentences should get the job done.

The Square-Shaped Podcast Image

Your podcast is going to need a square-shaped image that represents your show on iTunes; this is a component of your podcast that you cannot avoid. However, our old friend Fiverr.com is a great resource if you're not a graphic artist or you don't trust a friend or family member to do it for you.

There are many free images to use on the internet, but you must make sure you have the rights to use it and modify it. You need to modify it because your image should have the text of your podcast name on it. This could be done in something as simple as Microsoft Paint, or something a little more advanced such as Microsoft Publisher, Adobe Photoshop, etc.

Just make sure that whoever designs your image uses the right pixel image size of 3000x3000, which are the latest specifications according to iTunes. Make sure it's visually appealing and has the name of your podcast on it. These images are important when people are searching for it on iTunes. The image will appear when people are searching for your podcast (or podcasts with similar keywords).

The image should be in a JPG or PNG format. The text should be large and legible, so the name of your podcast stands out.

Don't overthink this; don't overlook it either. You need an image, a title, and a description. When you are creating your SoundCloud account, you will enter this information under the *Edit Your Profile* link.

You will also add your podcast's official image in this part of SoundCloud.com too.

Inside SoundCloud, after you have logged in, you will click on the button that says *Edit*. This *Edit* button is located on the right side of your homepage on the SoundCloud screen, near the top of the page. It will have a little pencil icon located next to the word *Edit*. Click on this Edit button.

What will appear next is the *Edit your Profile* box. The title of your podcast will go underneath the *Display name* field. The square-shaped image that you've had created to represent your podcast should be added where it says *Update Image*.

The description of your podcast that will eventually appear

inside iTunes will go under the *Bio* field. After you have added a *Display Name, Image* and *Bio* inside the *Edit your Profile* section of SoundCloud, you will click the *Save Changes* button.

Remember that the major theme of this book is getting it Done is Better Than Perfect. You want your podcast out there because its content is great (and it's something the world ought to hear); don't get trapped in these stages of the process and overthink your image, description, etc.

These stages of creating a podcast are necessary but nowhere near as important as the content of your podcast. The authenticity of the conversations you begin to open up in the podcast is what the art is about.

Don't let these little speed bumps of coming up with a description, graphic, or how to edit it stop you. Freelance labor is everywhere. It can help you when you're "stuck." I always recommend Fiverr.com.

Or you can figure it out yourself; it just takes repetition, trial and error—you got this!

Alright, the next thing you need to do is get an RSS feed. Guess what? SoundCloud provides it for free!

Of course, if you want unlimited amounts of podcasting hours on SoundCloud, you'll have to upgrade to a Pro Account (roughly $150 a year) but the first couple hours of your podcast will be hosted for free.

To get your RSS feed from SoundCloud, simply navigate to *Settings* on the main screen of your SoundCloud homepage.

To get to *Settings,* you will click on the three dots located at the very top right-hand portion of this screen. The drop-down menu that appears underneath these three dots will include an option called *Settings* near the bottom.

Click on *Settings.* Within *Settings,* there will be a section labeled *Content* which you will click on.

This is where the URL of your RSS feed is located. Your RSS feed URL should start with something along the lines of:

http://feeds.soundcloud.com/users/

Highlight the entire URL of your RSS feed by clicking on it and dragging your cursor over it.

Then you will right-click on it and select *Copy.*

After you've copied your RSS Feed, go to the Apple Podcast Connect website, located here:

https://podcastsconnect.apple.com/my-podcasts/new-feed

[Enter your Apple ID and Password there, and if you don't have one you can get it free by signing up.]

Once you've signed in to Apple Podcast Connect, you will simply paste your RSS feed into the box that Apple provides for you.

The box to paste your RSS feed into will be located underneath where it says *URL.* Paste the URL of our RSS feed inside this field and then click *Validate* and *Submit*.

Remember it may take a couple days or even two weeks for the team at Apple to approve your podcast, so remain patient. You should receive an email from Apple once it's accepted. You can also check your favorite podcast apps on your smartphone to see if your show has been accepted. Just search for its title.

After your show has been accepted into iTunes, every time you upload a new MP3 file of a podcast episode to SoundCloud, it will automatically appear in iTunes. Your subscribers will get a notification each time.

The beauty of the process that I've outlined is that you don't have to pay any money to SoundCloud or Apple if you want to submit your podcast this way. Since the first few hours of your podcast are hosted for free on SoundCloud, you can really test the waters and see if you like how everything shakes out before you commit to the unlimited storage options.

I can't reiterate this enough: as a new podcaster you should use the free services because you're going to be able to see if you like the way these systems work. You'll also see if Apple is picking up your podcast in iTunes.

If you like what you are doing and how things are going, then you can move forward and buy the unlimited storage options for about $150 or so a year. Unlimited hosting may cost a little more than that or it may be a bit less, but those numbers are going to give you an idea.

As I said, it may take anywhere up to two weeks for iTunes

to accept your podcast. As long as you're giving it the old college effort and your podcast isn't some sort of virus or something crazy, you'll get accepted.

At this point, you might want to celebrate! Things are going to be awesome, because your podcast is almost officially out there and you've done all the legwork to get it accepted in iTunes/Apple Podcasts.

iTunes/Apple Podcasts is far and away the most popular place for folks to listen to podcasts.

After all, every new iPhone comes with the podcast app automatically installed on it. Your podcast will be at the fingertips of so many different people. This is where the opportunities and amazing connections you can make with the rest of the world can truly take place.

Now that your podcast is out there, you might want to consider a little word of mouth marketing.

CHAPTER 5
GROWING YOUR
PODCAST

In my humble opinion, I believe the best way to market your podcast is to use the word of mouth techniques.

When I was attending the Podcast Movement Conference this past summer (the world's largest podcast and podcaster meeting), I learned something interesting. Market research was conducted to explore why people weren't listening to podcasts. A top reason was that people didn't know how to find a podcast.

That's why the word of mouth technique is so important. If you're having a casual conversation with a friend, and they ask you, "how are things going?", or "how are you?"

Tell them you started a podcast.

Throw it out there. It's an interesting conversation piece. The fact that you're working on a podcast is more interesting than the weather, and it might even be more interesting than talking sports (especially if your team is hurting).

Then when the other person asks a little bit more about your podcast, ask if they want to see it. If they have an iPhone, you're in some serious luck, because unless they deleted it, they have the purple colored app with the lowercase "i" icon on it labeled *Podcasts*.

The iconic Apple Podcasts app logo

Have them bring up their iPhone and then scroll to their *Podcasts* app. Then once you're inside the Apple podcast app, search for your podcast. Look it up; once it's been accepted, it'll come up. Select your podcast and hit "subscribe", maybe even give it a 5-star review while you're there on their phone.

Then say, "yeah, here's my podcast, check it out." You can even start playing the first episode if they seem really interested. That person will probably be amazed, and you just got yourself a new subscriber.

Market research has told us that a lot of people don't know what the *Podcasts* app does; they don't know how to use it. It's super simple though.

If your friend is on an Android, go to wherever they get apps and download a podcast player (I prefer the "Overcast" podcast player), and search for your podcast. If it's in iTunes, it'll be there too. That is the easiest way to market your podcast, and anyone can do that in person.

It also helps combat what market researchers have identified as a major reason people don't listen to podcasts—they simply don't know where to find them.

A lot of people say you need to have a website with your podcast, but it's not necessary to get a podcast off the ground and to actually be a podcaster. A podcast is not required to have a website before it can be admitted to iTunes.

Creating a podcast can be defined by getting it into iTunes. That's how important it is. I also want to mention that in 2017, Apple re-branded the iTunes podcast directory as Apple podcasts. You might notice that I'm using these interchangeably because essentially they are the same thing. For the sake of simplicity, just think of iTunes as Apple

Podcasts.

The iconic purple icon is on every single iPhone. If someone is asking about your podcast and they have an iPhone or smartphone, take the time to show them how to subscribe to it or how to pull it up. It's pretty cool that the algorithm in the iTunes search engine is so friendly to new podcasts. When you start typing in the name of your podcast, it's going to come up.

Remember when you had that square image created for your podcast so you could submit it to iTunes? That image is the first thing your friend is going to see when they search for your podcast, so make sure that image was done well.

Of course, you can always redo that image and resubmit it.

I do recommend that you create a website at some point if you have a long-term vision for your podcast.

While you don't need to have a website to get your podcast off the ground, a website is a great way to give people a call to action. When you're trying to promote your podcast, it's best to have a simple and easy-to-remember location to send people to listen to it. An easy-to-remember website name is where you can send them.

If you have a catchy URL, such as ComedyTravelPodcast.com, that's a really easy call to action for people to remember. You can't really send someone to the iTunes search bar as a call to action, it's not that easy to remember, but if you have a website, you (or your webmaster) can embed your podcast's feed into your website quite easily. You'll be able to do this through the tools provided by SoundCloud, Podbean, Libsyn, etc.

While it's really easy to link to your podcast within a social media post, that doesn't help you in a word of mouth situation. If you're in conversation with someone, it's not so simple. If you just want to tell someone how they can find your podcast, and you don't have time to pull it up for them, a website is a great call to action.

"Just visit my website to check out the podcast, Larry. That's ComedyTravelPodcast.com" (assuming you have a friend named Larry).

That's the number one reason why I recommend a website, but Search Engine Optimization (SEO) is another great reason to have a website. This will allow you to promote your podcast organically through SEO techniques. We could talk at length about how to do this but it's not within the scope of trying to launch a podcast. It's just something to keep in mind as your podcasting gains momentum.

With a website, you'll also be able to utilize Google Ad Words marketing campaigns if you really want to get your podcast heard and you have a budget. Of course, without a website, you could promote your podcast through a Facebook business account (free) and use the robust advertisement features offered by Facebook (not free) to promote it.

Again, that is pretty advanced stuff for a beginner so I wouldn't worry about it until later on when you're ready to explore more options to market your podcast.

The main reason that I like having a website is that you can tell people in a simple way where to go to hear your podcast.

When it comes to making a website, Squarespace, Wix or WordPress are going to get the job done. These are all great options if you want to get serious about building your podcast's website out.

If you just want to get a website up and running, I really recommend Wix.com or Squarespace.com, because you can create the website without having to buy it first. With Wix.com, you can create the whole website and then once you really like it, you can buy it. With WordPress, you're going to get so much more out of it in the long run, but you're going to have to buy it up front (before you see what it will look like).

There are endless amounts of videos and instructions to watch on how to use these tools, but put these options in your back pocket and save them for a time when you're more established. Creating a website is essential if you're serious about taking your podcast to the next level, but it's not necessary when trying to get a podcast started.

If down the line you want to build some premium subscription options for your website and podcast, you'll want to use WordPress. Having premium content is a way to monetize your podcast which is a major subject that comes up a lot in the podcast universe.

CHAPTER 6
MONETIZING YOUR
PODCAST

People want to figure out how to cash in with a podcast. I'm going to be brutally honest with you; if money is the only reason why you want to start a podcast, it's a bad motive. Deriving revenue from a podcast is a significant challenge, and I believe money alone should not be the reason to make podcasts.

I'm not telling you to not dream big dreams, but a podcast is not a get-rich-quick scheme. A podcast is not your ticket to the end of any financial woes.

Being authentic and using it as a tool to make you happier is the key. Usually, when things are going well, and it's making you happy, the next thing you know is, it's growing an audience. The audience could be huge someday. At that point, you can begin to think about monetizing it, because of how huge the audience has grown.

Make podcasts to get stories, opinions and analysis out there. You want to bring what's unique about you to the rest of the world. Many people believe (including me) that podcasting is the most intimate of all media.

85% of podcasters aren't generating revenue according to RadioPublic CEO Jake Schapiro.

15 billion podcast downloads produced just $300 million in revenue. That's not a great ratio, but it also shows it's possible to get paid from a podcast.

It's definitely not the "low-hanging fruit" when it comes to getting paid, but if you don't take no for an answer, and you want to make money podcasting, there are some things to remember.

There are ways to make money from a podcast, including some unique ways you probably weren't thinking about.

Let's review.

Advertising

The most traditional way to monetize a podcast is through selling ads. Getting someone to pay you to read an advertisement of theirs on your podcast is the most common route to getting paid.

You must prove to the advertiser that people are listening to make this happen. That's why you need reliable metrics.

This is also why you need to have a premium account with podcast hosting services such as SoundCloud, Libsyn, Podbean or Blubrry.

The reliable metrics that you will get on who is listening to your podcast is one of the most valuable aspects of using these podcast hosting services.

These metrics will give you an idea of who is listening to your show, what part of the world they're listening from, and what devices they use to listen. It's really crucial for the advertiser to know these facts before they commit to paying you.

How do you get advertisers? Relationships are probably the best way. An ideal situation is if you can prove that your podcast is being listened to, and you know someone (or someone who knows someone) that might be interested in advertising.

Approach them with an email. You have to work really hard to sell your podcast to advertisers. You have to search out contact information of people that might be interested in advertising. You have to be really resilient.

It's a major skill set that involves having a thick skin and bouncing back from rejection. Most importantly, you have to build up a substantial audience before you can really approach advertisers with any sort of leverage.

If you're serious about cashing in, there are other ways to make podcasting money besides advertising.

Affiliate Marketing

You can get referral sponsorships as part of an affiliate marketing plan. This is a great way to make money from a podcast, but again it relies on having an established audience first.

Affiliate marketing is a way to get a commission from the sales that you bring to another business. It's when you work with a brand to make sure you get compensated for whatever business you can prove you are sending their way.

For example, say you have a partnership with Airbnb. If their customers are using the promo code you promoted on your podcast; then you get paid a percentage of however much money they spend with your promo code.

It's typically the second most popular way people make money from podcasts after traditional advertising. Having these referral relationships with brands, rather than just a straight up advertising relationship, can prove really profitable.

I do want to reiterate that you have to have a really large audience established. The way to get that audience established is by being you. Let your podcast grow organically; don't go into it with the mindset that you're only in it to make money.

Going into podcasting with the mindset that you're there to tell beautiful stories and to bring what's unique about your experience in this life to the world is a better idea.

Everyone has their independent story. Let your podcast be your outlet for getting it out there. Share your expertise with the world. Share that hidden talent and do it through a podcast.

A Self-Published Book

It might be time to consider self-publishing a book once you have enough quality podcasts made.

You've told a bunch of great stories, had many great interviews and things are going well. So now there's a way you can create a new medium from your podcast.

Take all the MP3 files of your favorite episodes and send them to Speechpad.com. (Again I don't get paid by any of these websites, I just tell them to you because I believe in them.)

Speechpad.com is a fast and affordable transcription service. It will take all those MP3 files and put them into transcriptions.

Next, you will take those transcriptions and send them to a copy-editor that you've hired on Fivver.com or Upwork.com.

Tell the copy-editor the specifics of what you want. For a few hundred dollars of the transcription service and the use of the freelance talent, they will help put all that stuff together for you into a book.

You can then self-publish that book on Amazon for free.

By self-publishing that book you have now become a published author. That's right. You can become a published author through your podcast.

Here's a step-by-step, rough blueprint for turning a podcast into a book.

1. After you've had the podcast established, make sure you've saved all those MP3 files that you're sending over to SoundCloud and submit them to Speechpad.com. Speechpad will charge you $1 for each minute of audio to be transcribed. (The price could end up being a little more or less, but this gives you a general idea).
2. When those transcriptions come back to you, copy and paste them together and add some additional commentary to connect everything together. You should consider adding an introduction before each episode.
3. Next, you will create a free account on Kindle Direct Publishing, a service of Amazon which will offer you plenty of free templates to lay out the interior of your book.
4. Utilize a freelance graphic artist on Fiverr.com to create your book cover.
5. Follow the steps on Kindle Direct Publishing to submit your book. Amazon will publish on-demand, and you will not be stuck with inventory! In return for their robust free services, Amazon will take a percentage of each book sold.

(I recommend taking the time to lay out your book on your own. If you teach yourself to be smart and resilient, and you take the time to do some of these jobs yourself, you can save a lot of money on freelance labor.)

You've just become a self-published author through your podcast! You're doing things that we never dreamed possible for a hobbyist to do 10 - 15 years ago.

The quality depends on you. However much work (and investment in freelance labor) you put into it will generally determine how much quality the book ends up having. High quality is nice, but in my opinion, done is always better than perfect.

You will continue to gain momentum from the effort that you're putting forth. All of these audio files that you're creating in your podcast can be transcribed into a book. Furthermore, it doesn't cost overhead money to have this book on Amazon. What a time to be podcasting!

Selling a book of glorified podcast transcripts is another way to monetize things that a lot of people don't think about. A lot of people aren't doing it. You have to think creatively with these podcasts. Good things are going to happen with effort and doing what you love (podcasting). Fortune ends up breaking for those that work the hardest. I'll just leave this here…

"I'm a great believer in luck, and I find the harder I work the more I have of it."
   -Thomas Jefferson

A Tool in the Marketing Toolbox

A podcast alone isn't a great way to make money, but it can be a tool in your marketing toolbox. It's a great way to expand your brand. For example, say you already have a blog. Most likely, blog content can easily be transferred into a podcast.

Your blogs can be read by a voice-over artist that you can hire from Voices.com or Voices123.com. A professional with a beautiful voice can read your blog content, and you can put it out as a podcast. (Or of course you can just read it yourself too.)

A podcast can be a major tool in your marketing toolbox. Just don't look at a podcast as the only way for you to bring in money, because you'll probably be disappointed.

Content Marketing

If you work at a company, don't be afraid to encourage your boss to start a podcast for the company. It will look especially attractive if you take him or her through the process. The startup costs of podcasting are way below the costs of many other marketing strategies. This alone could entice them to launch it.

Show them the measly startup costs and describe the incredible amounts of exposure and potential business it can bring to your company if you make it interesting, and it gets hot.

Of course, for it to get hot, you have to make it compelling.

A problem will arise with a brand podcasting when they make it sound too much like advertising copy. If a business decides to podcast, it has to be an example of content marketing.

Content marketing involves talking about topics around what your product is, or what you're trying to sell, while at the same time not just blindly trying to sell your product.

For example, if you own an auto mechanic shop in the middle of Maryland, talk about the top ten reasons why mufflers go bad.

Have the podcast be about interviewing an expert on mufflers. Talk about what's wrong with them. Perhaps your shop sells auto parts too. At the end of the podcast episode, mention that you own a shop, and you have a website. Folks can learn more by visiting the website, or the shop.

That's the essence of content marketing. It's about giving something of value with your content, and then giving a call to action at the end. The content is what people value and what will attract them to your business. That's why they call it "in-bound marketing."

People want realness. People want authenticity. If you want to do this right, you have to be in it for the long run. Don't just try to trick people with clickbait or SEO gimmicks. If your company is going to have a podcast, it has to be interesting and also related to what you sell.

It's another way that you can monetize a podcast.

If you work for a company, suggest to them you start a podcast. You could even be the host. You've read this book. You know enough to do it! If you have a friend that owns a business, tell them that you'll do a podcast for them for free. Maybe it could lead to some compensation down the line for you.

These are the efforts that you have to make. They can open up opportunities for you that you never dreamed possible.

If you're going to make a mistake, make it because you worked hard and it didn't work out. Don't make a mistake because you were too lazy to try. It's much harder to live with the latter for me.

It's okay if the podcast doesn't end up being what you thought it was going to be, but please, don't be scared to try it.

Tell someone you know, "Hey, I can create a podcast for your business."

That's a way to monetize a podcast that I don't think a lot of people think about. If you're going to make a mistake with podcasting, make a mistake because your audio ended up stinking or you had too many "Popping P's" muffling your audio track.

Don't make a mistake because you didn't try, because you can still self-publish a book with that low-quality audio, and it still might sound amazing on paper.

Good luck and happy podcasting.

CHAPTER 7
HAPPY PODCASTING

You've made a great decision to get involved with a podcast. With Google, the amount of information out there on how to make it great is endless.

Like I mentioned in the opening of this book, just keep trying to get it out there. The more you try, the more you learn.

There's something so powerful that happens when you actually decide to get something done, rather than continuously read about how to do it, or endlessly brainstorm/map out how to do it. Don't get me wrong, you do want to prepare, but ultimately you have to just do it like Nike.

Open up that laptop. Open up Audacity. Hit record. Edit that sucker and put it out there. Now it's out there to the world. Who knows who's going to hear it? You won't know. Say you're a shy comedian that just wants to get jokes out there; it could be Judd Apatow listening. You just never know!

To get feedback on your podcast, have a clear way for people to reach you. You want to get feedback. Have an easy-to-remember Twitter handle. Tell them to tweet you at @ComedyTravelerPodcast (for example); or whatever your easy-to-remember Twitter handle is.

Have a public Twitter account because Twitter and podcasting tend to go well together.

Make sure folks can reach you because you want to get feedback, and you want to open up network connections. Leave an email address (email accounts are free).

It's so crucial to get feedback on what you're doing. If you tell your story, or you have a guest tell their story, and you get really open, honest and vulnerable, the sky is the limit. You might make a connection with someone that you never dreamed possible. Your life could dramatically change for the better.

Life and podcasting are so unexpected, but don't come into your podcast with expectations of cashing in on it. Be open-minded and commit to being honest and authentic. Dedicate yourself to telling stories that you want the world to hear. Use it to say the things you want to say, and interview the people you want to interview. Be excited about the endless possibilities.

Whether it's through people finding you, or connecting with old friends, use these revealing long-form interviews to open relationships with a podcast. If you do it right, your life could change for the better, simply because you make the efforts.

You are putting yourself in a situation where your life can change for an unimaginably better future. I truly believe making effort is what this digital world thrives upon. It's about getting your content out there on the Internet. Countless amounts of eyes are waiting as long as you continue to make it authentic.

I'd be remiss if I didn't mention the fact that I couldn't have written this book without the knowledge I gained at the Podcast Movement Conference.

No matter what level of podcasting you find yourself at, everyone—even if you are simply "thinking" about starting a podcast—should try to attend. The conference is something that I've mentioned in this book a few times. It's the world's largest podcasting conference.

Again, I'm not paid to mention the conference, I just believe in the power of its supportive community and all the amazing knowledge they opened my eyes to. It was inspiring.

If you can afford it, or maybe if it's in your area, I highly recommend going. The community of podcasters that you are going to meet are extremely interesting and supportive.

You're going to meet some of the most profitable and prolific podcasters in the world. On the flipside, you're going to meet people who are just starting out, people who don't even have a podcast and just need a little encouragement to create one on their own.

If you get a chance to go to this conference, take advantage. Look it up on www.PodcastMovement.com, or search for it on Google.

On a final note, I want to leave you with some thoughts on a concept that comedian Joe Rogan calls "famine thinking." Rogan is arguably the world's best podcaster. *The Joe Rogan Experience* is perennially ranked in the top ten of the most listened-to podcasts in the world.

Rogan is highly critical of this mentality.

Famine thinking is when you view everyone and everything around you as competition. Instead of being inspired by other great artists, famine thinkers get competitive and worry that there aren't enough accolades left for them. You will most likely get discouraged from starting a podcast if you think this way.

An excuse that is often utilized to avoid starting a podcast is that "someone has already done it." This is a staple of famine thinking. The antidote to famine thinking is to gain inspiration from other great podcasters and learn from them. Be a fan. Make sure you look at greatness and derive happiness from it, not jealousy.

Pay attention to what other great podcasters are doing right and see what it is you can incorporate into your own style a little. You're not trying to copy them; you're evolving the medium by adding your unique voice and authenticity (that "you" factor) into something that already works. All great artists have influences.

Podcasters are a very supportive community. That's why there is no room for a *famine mentality* in this medium. Utilize the supportive nature of podcasting and grow your own show by requesting to be interviewed on other people's podcasts.

Being a fan is an important job of a podcaster! Listen to the shows that are similar to your podcast and search them out a little more on Google. Find where to contact them and let them know you'd love to be on their show to discuss X,Y and Z.

You'll quickly find that in podcasting; the top podcasters frequently appear on the other top podcasts. It's typically a reciprocal relationship; so feel free to invite ANYONE— even the top podcaster in the world—on your show. There is no downside in asking.

A podcast can be a way to make you happier right off the bat, so use it for that.

As I mentioned at the beginning of this book, a podcast is a new thing for you to do at night! As crazy as that might sound, think about it again. You have karaoke, dancing, bowling, dinner, movie and now podcasting!

Get your best friend over, crack open some beers or have a nice glass of wine on that Saturday night and podcast. Banter together over a topic, if you like. Just talk about what you want to talk about.

Tell people you have a podcast and ask if they want to come on it. Talk about that incredible road trip you took with each other in 1998 when you saw all 30 Major League Baseball stadiums. Just talk about it and see where it goes. You don't have to post it publicly, if it gets too personal.

Going down memory lane with your friend like that can rekindle relationships. A podcast can bring you closer to some of the most important people in your life. It can vividly help you remember why you love that friend so dearly.

You're telling incredible stories that have never been told before, and they will live on for generations. A podcast could be a great way for future generations of your family to learn about you.

Not only are you getting these stories off your chest, but you're also sharing them with the world, and that's really how a podcast can take off.

With the right mentality, I truly believe you will attain a great podcast and increase your overall happiness.

And in my humble opinion, that's the most important metric of all. Happy podcasting.

APPENDIX

Podcast Editorial Calendar

An editorial calendar can give your podcast some direction. It's a map of what subjects you want to cover on your podcast and when you plan to release new episodes to the public. **Here's an example:**

The Comedy Club Traveler's Guide Podcast - Editorial Calendar

Release Date	Episode Number	Episode Subject
Nov. 1, 2019	1	Trip Review – Thoughts on my recent trip to The Comedy Cellar in New York City.
Nov. 8, 2019	2	Interview – Chat with Vinnie Brand, owner of The Stress Factory Comedy Club in New Brunswick, N.J.
Nov. 15, 2019	3	Trip Review – Thoughts on my recent trip to Side Splitters Comedy Club in Tampa, Fla.
Nov. 22, 2019	4	Trip Review – Thoughts on my recent trip to The Comedy Store in Hollywood, Calif.
Nov. 29, 2019	5	Interview – Chat with legendary producer and comedic talent manager, Barry Katz.

How to use Audacity's Noise Reduction tool

Unless you have a recording studio, ambient background noises are most likely going to be a part of your podcast, but learning how to use the Noise Reduction Tool in Audacity will help immensely.

The Noise Reduction Tool is one of my favorite techniques to quickly improve the overall sound quality of a podcast. It can be utilized in the following steps:

- Open Audacity as if you were going to record a new podcast. Before your interview, make sure your microphone is plugged in and selected in Audacity's microphone drop-down menu.

- Before your podcast, record 5 straight seconds of background/ambient noises without anyone speaking into the microphone.

- After your podcast episode has concluded, highlight the five seconds of background/ambient noises that you recorded by selecting the "I" shaped Selection Tool (depending on what version of Audacity you are using, this Selection Tool is located above or next to the Zoom Tool, which is represented by the magnifying class icon).

- While left clicking your mouse, drag your cursor over the five seconds of background/ambient noises, and unclick the mouse when you're done highlighting the five seconds.

- Next, navigate your cursor to the top menu of Audacity and click on *Effect*. When the drop-down menu appears below *Effect*, click on *Noise Reduction*... When the Noise Reduction box opens, click on the button that says *Get Noise Profile*.

- Next, you will navigate your cursor to the top menu of Audacity and click on *Select*. When the drop-down menu appears below *Select*, click on *All*.

- Audacity has automatically selected all of the audio in your project. This is what we want!

- Once again, you will navigate your cursor to the top menu of Audacity and click on *Effect*. When the drop-down menu appears below *Effect*, click on *Noise Reduction*... When the Noise Reduction box opens, click on the button that says *OK*.

Audacity has automatically taken out the background/ambient noises from your entire recording. The magic of Audacity allows you to isolate the noise you don't want and through the steps I've outlined above, it takes it out of your entire project.

If this tool is too complicated for you to try to use, don't worry... maybe you can just turn that loud Air Conditioning unit off and reduce background noises the old fashioned way.

GLOSSARY

Audacity – Free audio-editing and recording software. Download Audacity as a simple and free way to record and edit your podcasts.

Fiverr.com – A website to find freelance workers to complete gigs for you, such as editing your podcast or creating the podcast's square-shaped image that appears in iTunes. Gigs on Fiverr start at just $5. Upwork.com is another popular website to find freelance workers.

iTunes/Apple Podcasts - Apple Podcasts is the app that most people use to locate, listen and subscribe to podcasts. iTunes is the directory for podcasts that you will submit your RSS feed to (see Chapter 4). It's imperative to get your podcast accepted by iTunes since it's the most popular place in the world for people to find podcasts.

LAME MP3 Encoder – This is a free software that will run unnoticed in your computer's background. You'll need to download this so Audacity can export what you've recorded in it to an MP3 file.

MP3 File – The end product of what you'll record in Audacity and export/save. You'll upload the MP3 file of each of your episodes into SoundCloud.com (or whatever podcast hosting service you choose to utilize).

MusicBakery.com – This is a website I recommend using to buy music to add to your podcast. What I like most about MusicBakery.com is that you buy the audio once and you can use it forever. Many other popular websites only allow you to use the music track one time after you buy it.

Podcast Movement Conference – Typically held in the summer in a different major American city each year. It's the largest gathering of podcasters and is essentially the Super Bowl of podcasting. It's great for seasoned podcast professionals, or for someone who's never podcasted but has an itch to start one.

Skype – Free software that will allow you to call anyone in the world with an internet connection. Learning how to use Skype is crucially important for those that want to interview people remotely.

Skype Number – This will allow people from anywhere in the world to call you on Skype from a cell phone or landline. It's ideal for recording remote podcast interviews when your guest is unfamiliar with using Skype. In the U.S., you may purchase a Skype number for roughly $55 per year.

SoundCloud – This is the free service that will host your podcast. It is also where you will get the URL of your RSS feed that you submit to iTunes (see Chapter 4). Logon to SoundCloud.com and create an account. The first 3 hours of your podcast will be free to host on SoundCloud.

You can upgrade to an Unlimited Pro Account for about $12 per month for unlimited amounts of hosting hours. Other popular podcast hosting services include Libsyn, Podbean and BluBrry.

Speechpad.com – This is a website where you can have your podcast episodes accurately transcribed for about $1 per minute of audio.

USB Microphone – This is a key element of an efficient podcast workflow. USB microphones are great because they plug directly into the USB port, which is universal to all computers and laptops. They range in price from about $20 to $200.

Popular USB microphones amongst podcasters include the Blue Snowball and Audio Technica AT2020.

VoiceMeeter – Free software that you'll download in order to record the sounds coming from your computer. You will need this if you choose to record a podcast with someone calling into your computer (via Skype) from a remote location. Don't worry about downloading it if you are not planning on interviewing people remotely.

REFERENCES

Allan, Patrick. (2017, August). *How to Start Your Own Podcast.* https://lifehacker.com/how-to-start-your-own-podcast-1709798447

Flynn, Pat. (2018, July). *How to Start a Podcast in 2018: Pat's Complete Step-By-Step Podcasting Tutorial – UPDATED!* www.smartpassiveincome.com/tutorials/start-podcast-pats-complete-step-step-podcasting-tutorial/

Gross, Terry (2018, July). *All I Did was Ask: An Afternoon with Terry Gross.* Session presented at Podcast Movement Conference.

Firemark, G., & Lieberman, J (2018, July). *Legal Issues for Podcasters and Content Creators.* Session presented at Podcast Movement Conference.

Rogan, Joe. (2014, January). *The Joe Rogan Experience: Episode 437*

Shapiro, Jake (2018, July). *The Missing Marketplace: Monetizing Podcasts Beyond the 1%.* Session presented at the Podcast Movement Conference.

ABOUT THE AUTHOR

Casey Callanan is the owner of Clear Contender Media. A company he started to further his life goals of helping the world communicate better. Casey is a graduate of West Virginia University's Reed School of Media. As a lifelong writer and boxing enthusiast, he believes the same principles that make a great prizefighter (perseverance, resilience, and the will to be great) translate rather perfectly to the world of podcasting.

As a successful podcast host with a background in journalism, communications and digital marketing, he's in the business of helping people communicate better one story at a time.

THANK YOU

I appreciate you taking the time to read this book. Starting a podcast is one of the most exciting and gratifying experiences of my life and I'm thrilled to share some tips, tricks and insight with you.

I'd love to hear from you. Feel free to leave a helpful review on Amazon, or find my contact information on **ClearContender.com** and drop me a line!

- Casey Callanan

Learn more at **ClearContender.com**

Made in the USA
Lexington, KY
08 January 2019